To Bryce, Landyn & Wyatt,

May all your dreams come true & your hearts always soar.

Kathryn

7-26-13
Old Faithful Inn
Yellowstone N.P.

A Goose Tale:
Gwen and Gabe's Journey

Written by **Kathryn Phyllarry**

Illustrated by **Robert Rath**

Homestead Publishing

Moose, WY • San Francisco, CA

In memory of my parents, Phyllis and Harry,
for whom I write.

Geese live exciting lives, you'll find,
not a life like yours or mine.

Copyright © 2010 by Kathryn Rittmueller

Book design by Robert Rath

All rights reserved. No part of this book may be reproduced or transmitted in any form or by any means, electronic or mechanical, including photocopying, recording or by any other information storage retrieval system, without written permission from the publisher.

ISBN 978-0-943972-82-4

Library of Congress Control Number 2010923394

First Edition
Printed in China

Published by
Homestead Publishing
Box 193 • Moose, Wyoming
& San Francisco, California

For other fine Homestead titles, please contact:
Mail Order Department
Homestead Publishing
Box 193 • Moose, Wyoming 83012
or www.homesteadpublishing.net

Gwen and Gabe arrived in Canada in early May,
and here for the summer they would stay.
After a long trip from New Mexico,
their migration route they already know.

To this lake, their parents brought their broods

because of good temperature, nesting and food.

Both Gwen and Gabe were one year old, and their
families they would leave to start one of their own.
When Gabe saw Gwen, his heart soared like a kite;
you could definitely say it was love at first sight.

For a nesting site they looked a lot,

    but they just couldn't find the perfect spot.

  "This lake is too crowded, Eh?" Gwen confided.

    So they'd go to a different lake they decided.

To a smaller lake a mile away,

    they would look for a nest most of the day.

When suddenly they found the spot that was best

    to settle in and make their nest.

Their nest of plants, feathers and grass

was built strong and sturdy so that it would last.

In the middle of May,

five eggs Gwen would lay.

Gabe guarded the nest

and sat on the eggs to give Gwen a rest.

Into the lake, Gwen would go for a snack

but not for long, she'd hurry back.

In about four weeks,
    the goslings broke through their eggs
    and quickly stood on their little legs.

Then Gwen and Gabe took their brood for a swim around the lake, staying close to its rim.

The next day Gwen said;

"Gabe, we need to move the goslings

to a place where they'll be well fed."

Gabe responded; "You betcha, for sure."
And he set out on a fatherly tour.

Since Gabe was molting and couldn't fly,

    he had to walk, not take to the sky.

Around the lake, Gabe began to waddle,

    he wasted no time, and he didn't dawdle.

Gwen would begin molting by the end of June,

    so he needed to find a new home very soon.

A secure place he would need to select,

    so he and Gwen, their brood could protect.

Gwen and Gabe's feathers would grow back in thirty days.

    Then they could get back to their flying goose ways.

It took quite a while,

    but Gabe found a spot that was right;

    it had lots of food and protection in the night.

A small mossy overhang at the south edge of the lake

    would be the perfect place for a summer home to make.

As Gabe led the way and Gwen brought up the rear,

in a straight line their goslings they steered.

To the mossy overhang they brought their brood,
  to spend the summer with plenty of food.
While Gwen and Gabe got new feathers,
  and the goslings learned how to fly,
    they would watch for danger with a cautious eye.

The goslings would eat all the time;
   it was good that this area had many places to dine.
On land or in the water, the goslings could eat all day;
   the abundance of food never seems to go away.
It's a land of berries, grass, corn and wild barley;
   these are just a few foods on which geese can parlay.

Then, with heads in the water,

    which makes them seem like they're hiding,

        on the bottom of the lake, their bills they are sliding.

This shovel-like motion was used to the hilt

    to stir up the precious food-laden silt.

Also on the lake bottom the goslings found

    that eel grass, sea lettuce and sargasso abound.

Gwen taught the brood to use their feathers as a tool;

if they flattened them out, they'd stay very cool.

Then Gabe was the teacher on how to stay warm —

by fluffing one's feathers against a harsh storm.

A family of snow geese lived down the shoreline;
   when Gwen counted, their number was nine.
They were from French Canada and had feathers of white,
   and they kept to themselves which just wasn't right.
His name was Nick and his mate Lynsette.
   And did they think they were special? Oh, you bet!

They waddled around with their bills in the air;
Nick and Lynsette were quite a pair.

One night, when Gwen and the goslings were asleep,

Gabe suddenly whispered, "Don't say a peep."

His keen sense of hearing warned of danger out there,

and Gabe and Gwen knew they needed to be aware.

Gwen lowered her body and stretched out her wings and neck to cover the goslings, the best way she could to protect.

Gabe quietly swam to the middle of the lake

to get a better view of the danger at stake.

In an instant the snow geese sent out an alarm,

hissing and honking, their brood was in harm.

A wily skunk pair, looking for food,

made a late night attack on Lynsette and Nick's brood.

Gabe quickly came to help Nick in the fight.

The two flapped, bit and hissed with all of their might.

But the spray was too smelly,

and the skunk's were too quick;

it was a terrible night for Lynsette and Nick.

Gabe was not hurt too bad. He just felt very, very sad.

The snow geese had scattered, and he didn't know their fate.

He felt he had arrived too late.

Gabe limped back to Gwen in the middle of the night and told her about Lynsette and Nick's plight.

Gabe smelled like skunk from head to webbed feet,

but Gwen and the goslings he was happy to greet.

Cautiously, at dawn the next day,

Gwen and Gabe took the goslings

into the lake for some play.

Gwen saw something white in the sun's morning glow

at the edge of the lake where the cattails grow.

As Gabe watched the goslings, Gwen swam to the site and found Lynsette shivering with fright.

Nick was close by in a somber mood;
only one gosling survived in their brood.

With one wing around the gosling

    and one around Lynsette,

        Gwen held them as close as a strong secure net.

Then Nick swam over and joined the troop.

    It certainly was a sad little group.

As the foursome slowly swam out of the weeds,
   other geese stopped their morning feeds.
To the snow geese, they swam with hurried feet
   to sincerely give a warm concerned greet.

Gabe and Gwen helped the snow geese find a new home just a short distance from their own.

As the summer went on, Nick and Lynsette made friends,

in spite of their differences, they made amends.

The weather got colder in early fall,
and all of the geese heard nature's call.

Gabe and Gwen asked the snow geese if they wanted to go
　　with them and their brood to New Mexico.
"Oui, Oui," was the answer Lynsette and Nick gave;
　　a new path in life, they wanted to pave.

The next day the geese took to the sky

for the long southward journey over many states to fly.

In a V-formation, Gabe took the lead,

but Gwen took her turn when she saw the need.

On the back of the V, the goslings you'd see.

This position the younger geese had,

so the long tiring flight wouldn't be so bad.

They would fly for fourteen hours a day

which is a very, very long time, Eh?

And they'd reach speeds up to 60 miles per hour;

I think you could say they had a lot of power.

Some days, the group would take a rest,
and in a corn field, they'd be a guest.

Then it was back to the sky on their southward quest
to a warmer place where the winters were best.

Over southern Wyoming, Gabe picked up the pace;
   it was like he was in a very fast race.
His parents had warned him of hunters below,
   and this was a caution every goose had to know.
"Avoid the James Gang whatever the cost,
   or your life may be lost!"

"Slow down ya goof," Gwen complained.

"This kind of speed, the flock can't sustain!"

Shots rang out and several wing feathers Gwen lost,
> and she quickly decided that Gabe was the boss.
Geese have ten kinds of calls,
> and Gwen said all ten without any stalls.

After several weeks on their migratory flight,
Northern New Mexico was finally in sight.

The flock saw what they thought

was a great winter spot,

but when dogs started chasing them,

they found it was not.

Then Gwen eyed a lake with food and protection

and thought it deserved further inspection

They finally decided this lake was the best;

it was much safer than all of the rest.

Through the winter, the goslings grew big and strong
and wouldn't be with their parents for long.

Early May, in Canada, the flock arrived,

    and throughout the summer, they would thrive.

The goslings left to find mates of their own

    and build a nest that they could call home.

Gwen and Gabe started a family all over again,

and a new set of goslings, they would defend.

With a cautious eye, Lynsette and Nick did the same,
and for all of their goslings to survive was their aim.

Thus the migration goes on year after year

    with one brood after another their parents to steer.

When in the sky honking you hear,

    look up, smile and have no fear.

Just wave and give a great big "HI"

    to the mighty geese as they fly by.

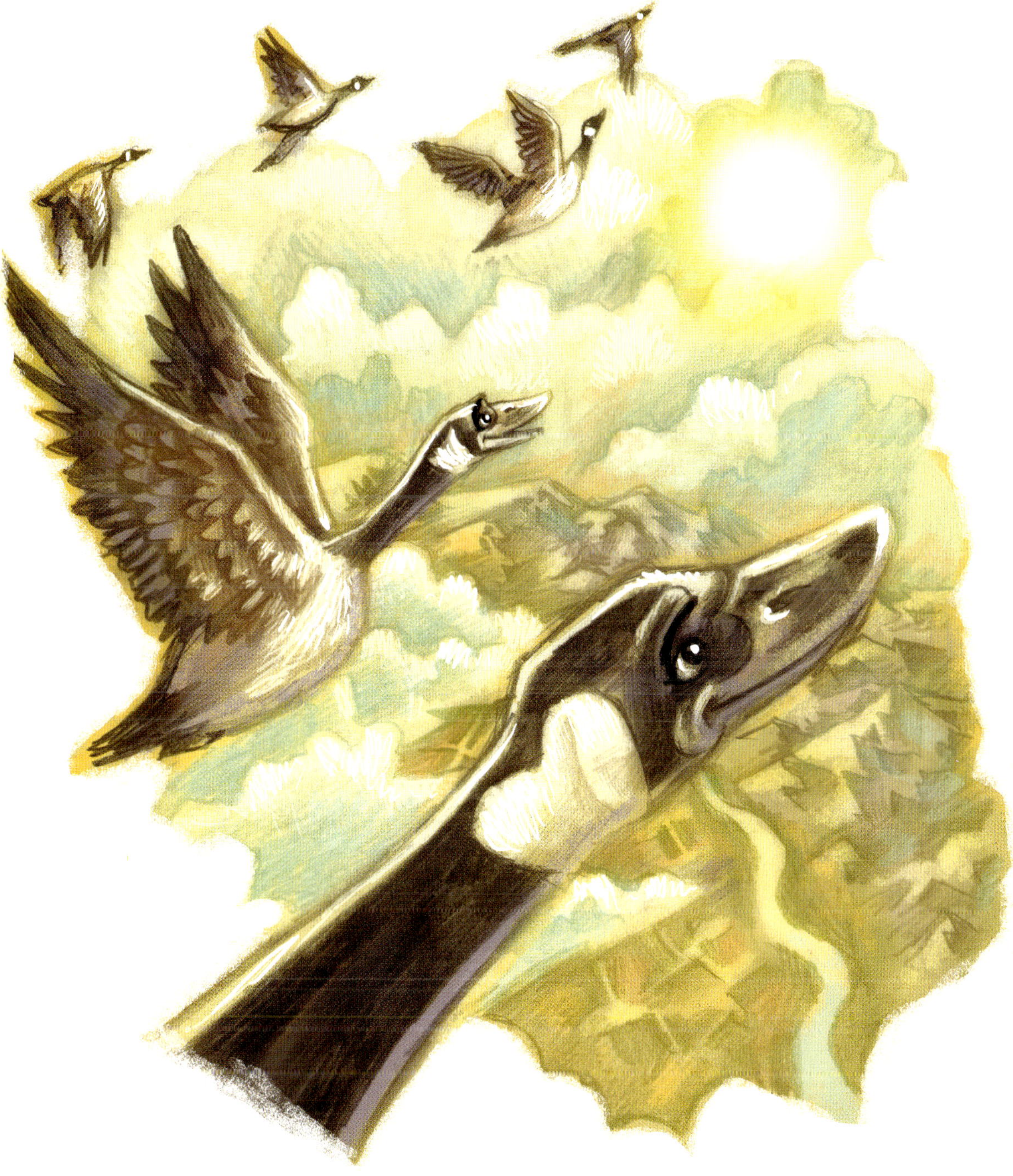

Kathryn (Jensen) Rittmueller, whose pseudonym is Kathryn Phyllarry, has lived in Wyoming for more than 30 years. Her first book, *Beauregart the Bear*, won a 2009 Moonbeam Award.